T0380872

Intoxicating Allure

To order additional copies of this book, contact:
Xlibris Corporation
1-888-795-4274
www.Xlibris.com
Orders@Xlibris.com

Vivette Davson aka Deepblaqsoul is at your personal intersection. I am delivering once again some of my exotic poetry with a dynamic turn. I aim to heat up your sheets and intoxicate you with my sultry allure. Run your fingers through these pages and soak up my seductive edge. Thanks for stopping by. Indulge as I pour on the heat. This is the beginning of the CHRONICLES OF DEEPBLAQSOUL.

STEAMY   STEAMY   STEAMY..............

Table of Contents

Naughty Naughty

I GOT A NAUGHTY NAUGHTY FOR YA
THIS EVENING U CAN BE OUTSPOKEN

IF I DON'T FINISH MY TEMPTATION ON THE WEB
U CAN HANG OUT WITH A SPOKENWORD CELEB

I WILL BE MUCH MORE PLEASING
WHEN I AM SETTLED DOWN
THEN I CAN FREAK YA MILDLY
OR JUST BE A PLAIN OLE CLOWN

SEXING YOUR MIND IS TURNING ME ON
U GOT ME USING FRENCH WORDS LIKE
BON BON

WHY ARE U DRIPPING CARAMEL COATED WORDS
TO MAKE ME WANNA LIFT MY SKIRT
I KNOW A LITTLE PEEK BABY WON'T HURT

NOW CHECK THE MESS U GOT ME IN
U STARTED THIS NOW TAKE IT TO THE FIN

JUICY TUNNELS ARE RUNNING BELOW
CANDIE SWEETIES AWAIT YOUR LIP SHOW
U NAUGHTY YA KNOW

Poetic Skills With Exotic Thrills

SEEKING THE GOOD LIFE THROUGH POETIC SKILLS
LOOKING FOR SENSUALLY EXOTIC THRILLS

WITH HEATED BLOOD FLOWING THROUGH MY VEINS
AND EXCITING MY BRAINS
EMITTING PROSE
THAT I COMPOSE

SPILLING AND SPITTING OUT LYRICAL ENERGY
WRAPPING WORDS IN TWOS
AND GIVING U CLUES
AS TO WHOSE MESSAGES I AM DELIVERING

WITH NO SPILLAGE
I COME GIVING YOU ALL A FULL DOSE
OF OVERSIZED PROSE
THAT I CHOSE
I SUPPOSE
I AM THE ONLY ONE WHO KNOWS
THE BEAUTY OF HEAVEN THAT LIVES WITHIN

Private Studio

LET ME BREAK DOWN MY BODY PARTS

THAT MIGHT TICKLE U FOR A START

B - IS FOR U TO BREAK IT DOWN BROTHER

O - IS FOR THE OPPORTUNITY TO EXPLORE ME LIKE NO OTHER

D - IS FOR SINKING DEEP BETWEEN MY HIPS

Y - IS FOR U TO TASTE THE SWEETEST LIPS YET

P - PLEASE ME WITH YOUR ROMANTIC WAND

A - AMPLIFY YOUR THRUST IF U MUST

R - IF THE TIME IS RIGHT U CAN UNWRAP YOUR GIFT

T - THANKS FOR THE TEASING AND THE TEMPTING

S - GO AHEAD AND CARESS ALL OF ME IN SLOW MO.....TION

BABY I HOPE U GET WHERE I AM COMING FROM

Putting an APB Out On U Baby

I AM DOING AN APB ON U HONEY
LOOKING FOR A MAN THAT COULD ENTICE ME
GIVING ME ALL THE CODES EVEN THE 911
OR THE SOS OR THE 411
THERE IS A JACKPOT TO BE WON

HIT A SISTER UP WITH SOME SUP
SNUGGLE UP TO ME BABY PUP
I NEED SOMETHING WITH A LITTLE MEAT
GUARANTEED TO MAKE MY TEMPERATURE RISE
CAUSE HE WILL HAVE TERRIFIC HEAT
IN RETURN I WILL DELIVER A FINE TREAT

HIT ME UP WITH SOME SOUL POETRY
SO WE CAN TRIGGER SOME NEW ENERGY
U SEE WE WILL HAVE A THANG GOING ON
FROM DUSK TILL DAWN

RUB A LITTLE SENTIMENT IN MY EAR
SPEAK SOFTLY
THEN WE CAN COMPARE
ALL THE SPICY LOVE NOTES
THAT KEEP US AFLOAT
I AM SO READY TO ROW YOUR BOAT

ARE U READY TO GET DOWN
ARE U READY TO GO UPTOWN
MY SIREEN WILL BE SCREAMING
DON'T STOP CHECKING MY 411
YOUR OPERATOR IS WAITING TO BREAK DOWN
REDIAL 911
GET UP GET READY TO THROW DOWN

Lover's Paradise

LAYING IN A POOL OF FLOWER PETALS
MY BRONZE BODY GLOWING LIKE OLYMPIC MEDALS

I AM YOUR PRIZE FOR ETERNITY
GIVING YOU WHAT U DESERVE MAGICALLY

HUGGING MY POWERED PILLOW
HEART THROBBNG SLOWLY
I FEEL MELLOW

DARLING I PLAN TO GIVE U A NIGHT U WILL NEVER FORGET
REMINISING OF THE CHEMISTRY WE FELT
WHEN WE FIRST MET

TOUCH ME
KISS ME
CARESS ME
HUG ME
COME CLOSE TO ME
AND THEN COME INTO ME

NEVER LET ME STOP BEING ADDICTED TO U HONEY
THESE CHAMPAGNE BUBBLES ARE POPPING ONE BY ONE
AS MY LOVE KEEPS POURING DOWN

YOU DRINK FROM MY FOUNTAIN AND I FILL YOU UP
WITH A FEELING THAT IS SO NICE
ENJOYING THE TOUCH OF LOVER'S PARADISE

Secret Chambers

I AM INVITING U INTO MY SECRET CHAMBERS
THEY SPREW FROM MY FINGERTIPS
IGNITING THESE COMPUTER CHIPS
I WANT U TO ENJOY THIS COURTSHIP
BECAUSE THE VIEW IS NAUGHTY AND EXOTIC

I WANT TO OPTOMIZE MY EFFECTIVENESS
NOT ONLY ON LINE
DO CALL ME TONITE
AND WE CAN SET IT OFF (OFF LINE)

I AM ENJOYING THIS RELATIONSHIP IMMENSELY
AND U ARE HEATING UP MY SURFACE INTENSELY

IF WE KEEP UP THIS ONE ON ONE
THE NEXT EPISODES WILL BE FUN

I AM ALWAYS THRILLED TO MASSAGE YOUR MIND
AND IF U NEED A LIFT
I PROMISE TO POUR OUT ON U
LIKE FINE CALIFORNIA WINE

TODAY I AM CAREFREE
AND I WOULD LOVE TO SHARE IT WITH U
HERE IS A HINT TO SATISFY YOUR VIEW

I AM GONNA CATER TO YOUR MOODS
FEEL FREE TO CHOOSE FROM MY ARRAY OF SOUL FOODS

1ST COURSE IS A MOUTH WATERING SALAD
FRENCHING ALL THE WAY
HOT BUTTERED BUNS
ASKING U TO STAY
A MAIN COURSE OF EXOTIC FISH
GARNISHING YOUR DISH
DESSERT IS A SWEET TART SHAPED LIKE A HEART
TOPPING OF THE NIGHT WITH U POPPING MY RED CHERRY
I KNOW U THINK I AM NAUGHTY
SO WHAT IF
U GET DRUNK ON ME HONEY
SO HOW ABOUT A CUP OF HOT STEAMY BLACK COFFEE

Sexual Satisfaction

AS I WRITE THESE LYRICS

I ANTICIPATE THE LAUGHS OR MAYBE THE KICKS

MY AUDIENCE WILL GET

AFTER I ALLOW THEM TO VIEW SOME OF MY PERSONAL FLICKS

INSIDE MY HEAD

BUT INSTEAD

I WILL STOP REWIND

AND GIVE A CLOSE UP VIEW OF MY MIND

HERE GOES MY IMAGINERY THEME

SOME MAY SAY

A DAY DREAM

BECAUSE THIS IS A FIGMENT OF MY MIND

I CAN CHANGE THIS PICTURE ANYTIME

LIKE I SAID BEFORE

IF THE EPISODES GET JUICY

PRESS FORWARD OR REWIND

THIS IS MY MEAL AND I AM ABOUT TO DINE

THEN WE CAN PAUSE

FOR THE RIGHT CAUSE

BECAUSE

THESE ARE THE LAWS

OF MY EXOTIC FIND

FOR NOW MY NEED IS SEXUAL SATISFACTION

I WILL SETTLE FOR THE DREAM

BECAUSE IT SATISFIES MY

FANTASY ATTRACTION

Episode 1

1ˢᵀ I WOULD LIKE TO TASTE U LIKE A MEAL
GEE WHIZ
I KNOW I AM ABOUT TO STEAL
THE CUTEST NIGHT
FROM THE FILES OF MY FANTASY
NOW LET US TAKE IT A STEP BACK
BEFORE THE CLIMAX & THE ECSTASY

Episode 2

I NEED TO SHOW CASE MY 5'9"
AS U SHOW OFF YOUR 6 9
GODDAMMIT BROTHER U ARE SO FINE
I WILL POP U LIKE A CHERRY
BUT NOT YET
I HAVE GOT TO MAKE U SWEAT

Episode 3

MY DESIRE, IS FOR U TO REKINDLE MY FIRE
BY TOUCHING MY TEXTURE
THEN I WILL GESTURE
AS TO OUR NEXT MOVE
THAT WILL PROMPT ME
TO NIBBLE ON YOUR NIPPLES
THAT WILL ULTIMATELY SEND WAVES AND BUBBLES
THROUGH YOUR BLOOD
LIKE A FLOOD
YOUR WAVES WILL RISE AND FALL

LIKE THE BREATHS WE BOTH TAKE
AS WE PARTAKE
TO SURF UP & DOWN DEEP VALLEYS
& YOUR SUGAR COATED HILLS
THAT WILL EVENTUALLY FILL
THEN BURST
LIKE POP CORN
YOU CANNOT WAIT TO POUR ALL THAT BUTTER
ALL OVER MY TRIANGULAR PASTURE
LIKE PINEAPPLE U DRIP ALL OVER ME

AS I VIEW YOUR CANDY CANE
ON THE 2ND RISE
I CAN'T HELP BUT CRAVE FOR
YOUR BEAUTY ONCE AGAIN

YOU KISS ME ON MY LIPS
THAT TASTE LIKE TOFFEE
I MUST ADMIT
I CAN BARELY CONTAIN MYSELF
AS I ADMIRE YOUR FINE SILHOUETTE
WHICH IS FINER THAN DARK COFFEE

I HAVE GOT TO TELL YOU BROTHER
U JUST BROKE MY CODES
THAT TRIGGERED A HEAT WAVE
NOW U KNOW I CAN'T HELP MYSELF
I WILL FOREVER BE YOUR LOVE SLAVE

Shades of Candelite Emotions

YOU SHINE ON ME

AND I REFLECT

A HOT SATIN GLOW

YOU ARE INTO MY MIND

MY BODY AND MY SOUL FO SHO

I PEEL BACK A FEELING OF CONTENTMENT

AS YOUR EMOTIONS CARESS MY THOUGHTS

I AM SO INTO YOU BABY

YOU ARE MAKING ME SO HAZY

A GOOD KINDA HAZY

ONE THAT MAKES ME CRAZY FOR YOU

AN IMAGINARY HUG IS ALL I NEED TODAY

TO START THIS LONG DISTANT FOREPLAY

THE RHYTHM IN MY STEP

IS BECAUSE YOU

HAVE KISSED MY SOUL

MY EBONY SKIN IS ON FIRE

EVERY TIME I DAY DREAM OF YOUR DESIRE

WE MOVE IN SYNC

BECAUSE YOU ARE MY NEW HEART BEAT

YOU BRING A SWEET MELODY WITH HEAT

YOUR ROMANITC WHIRLWIND WILL KEEP ME AFLOAT

BABY YOU ARE MY SUGAAH COATED MUSIC NOTE

YOU ARE THE BASS IN MY HEART

THE STRUM IN MY DRUM

THE MOAN IN MY SAXAPHONE

AND THE HYPNOTIC HUMM

BETWEEN MY LIPS

YOU ARE LIKE THE CHAMPAGNE BUBBLES

IN MY STOMACH JUST AFTER A FEW SIPS

YOU COLOR ME WITH A WILD STROKE

I LOVE IT WHEN YOUR PAINT BRUSH COVERS ME LIKE A CLOAK

I LOVE YOUR DESCRIPTION OF ME

AS HINTS COLORS AND HUES

I WAS SENT TO YOU BABY TO TAKE AWAY THE BLUES

MY SHADES WILL KEEP YOU COOL

AND I WILL KEEP YOU AFTER HOURS IN MY LOVE SCHOOL

I WILL MAKE YOU REPEAT MY LESSON

AFTER ALL THE PRACTICE YOU PUT IN

I CAN TELL YOU WILL BE A VETERAN

AFTER YOU TAKE ME TO THE FIN

WITH COUNTLESS LOVE MAKING

WE WILL BRING FORTH LITTLE BABY GIRLS AND BOYS FIT FOR OUR MISSIONS

DON'T EVER DROP OUT OF THESE SESSIONS

THERE IS A SPECIAL DAY SET ASIDE FOR GRADUATION

ALAS NO BRASS ON MY FINGER

A GOLD RING TO COMPLIMENT OUR LOVE FOREVER

A SYMBOL OF OUR HAPPINESS

ONLY WITH A STROKE FROM HEAVENS PALETTE

WE WILL BE BLESSED

GET DRESSED

IT IS OUR WEDDING DAY

SIGNATURE OF A DELUXE AFFAIR

MANY WILL STOP AND STARE

OOOO LA LA

WE WILL BE THE TALK OF THE TOWN

BABY DO HELP ME TO PUT ON MY CROWN

SEE WHAT YOU MADE ME DO

EVERYTIME I THINK OF YOU

XXXXXOOOOO

Sip My 4

THEN SIP MY 0

THEN AGAIN SIP MY 4

DRAW HARD ON THAT STRAW A 4

SWALLLOW TWO 1'S

THEN YOU ARE THIRSTY FOR ANOTHER 4

THEN LET ME TAKE YOU BACK TO 1

MY MY PUT YOUR TONGUE ON ANOTHER 1

LASTLY SMILE FOR THAT 1

YOU THOUGHT I WAS TRYING TO FREAK YA DELICATELY DIDN'T YA. WELL THAT SPELLS MY PHONE NUMBER 404 411 4111

Slipping From the Lip

SLIPPING FROM THE LIP

STRAIGHT TO THE HIP

FOR A TASTE OF EXOTIC

YOU KNOW IT IS GONNA BE A TRIP

NOT ONE OF THOSE LICKETY SPLIT

ONE THAT WILL BE TERRIBLY HECTIC

TAKE YOUR MEDICINE

YOU ARE NOT ALLOWED TO GET SICK

READY FOR THE RIDE

TILT SLIP AND SLIDE

OR IS IT DIP SLIP DRIP

LOLOL

I GOT MY ENGINE TURNED ON

THIS MORN

REMEMBER I AM SOFT ON THE WORDS

THE INTENT IS NOT PORN

JUST TRYING TO REBIRTH WORDS IN THEIR NATURAL FORM

THIS IS MEANT TO TURN YOU ON

Soothing Your Sensual Desire

I WANT TO SOOTH YOUR SENSUAL DESIRE
NOW IF YOU ARE HIPPED TO MY FLOW
MAY I GET PERMISSION
TO ATTACH TO YOU
WITH MY GLOW
IF U ONLY KNOW
WHAT LIES BENEATH MY MELANIN
U WOULD ADDRESS ME BEYOND THE BEAUTY OF THE SKIN

I ALWAYS GO DEEP DEEP WITHIN
SO PROMPT ME
AND HELP ME TO BRING OUT MY BEST

LET US WALK ON MY BEACH
AND LET ME TEACH CHA
HOW TO GUIDE MY EVERY MOVE
BY SLIDING UP AND DOWN MY HEATED GROOVES

SENSUALITY IS MY CLASS OF THE DAY
TANTALIZING IS THE MOOD I AM IN
I MUST SAY

I PLAN TO RUN MY HAND OVER YOUR LIPS
FEELING THE SOFTNESS AT MY FINGERTIPS
NERVES ON END
JUST WAITING FOR U TO RECOMMEND
WHICH WAY I SHOULD GO WITH THIS
A LITTLE KISS
A LITTLE KISS
LEADING TO A LITTLE THIS
AND A LITTLE THAT

BABY DO U COMPREHEND
MY LOVE LANGUAGE CODES
I LOVE ALLURE
AND FOR THIS
I AM SURE

Coming Attraction

IT IS SUMMER TIME

AND I AM THE NEW COMING ATTRACTION

AS THIS SCREENPLAY

OPENS TO DISPLAY MY ESSENCE

REVEALING ATTRACTIVELY

THE CUTEST V'S THAT

HOUSES ANCIENT RHYTHMS

ONLY ONE SPECIAL GENTLEMAN

CAN ENTER TO UNVEIL THIS COMING ATTRACTION

PULSATING

TANTALIZING

TITILATING

AND ENVIGORATING

HIS MOVES WILL BE TIMED

LIKE HEAT BENEATH MY SHEETS

AND MY LEGS WILL QUIVER AS HE GOES DEEP INTO MY STREAM

SQUIRTING CREAM

HIS HANDS WILL KISS MY CURVES

TINGLING MY NERVES

AND MAKING MY BODY DO SWERVES

OUR HEARTS WILL BE POUNDING AND

OUR BODIES WILL BE SOUNDING LIKE WAVES CRASHING

AGAINST A BEACH

AS WE REACH THE HIGHEST SENSUAL ECSTASY

AS HE PUTS A SILKY PLEASING ON ME

Too Steamy For U

LAYING HERE WAITING FOR U IS LIKE
WAITING FOR A CAR TO BE DETAILED
U HAVE NEVER FAILED
TO ENTICE ME
AGAIN AND AGAIN

AS U MOVE ALL UP INSIDE ME REAL SLOWLY
WITH YOUR WATER HITTING THE RIGHT SPOTS
U RUN ALL OVER ME CONTINUALLY
LIKE U ARE CONNECTING THE DOTS

U OCCASIONALLY PUT ON THE CHECK STOPS
FOR THE LAST TIME
I TELL U DO IT TIL MY KNEES DROP

U SLIDE AND GLIDE
ALL OVER MY BUMPER
WAXING MY UPPER AND MY LOWER

WE MOVE IN UNISON
U AND ME MR. JOHNSON

WITH YOUR WIPER BLADE U DO THAT SEDUCTIVE
BACK AND FORTH MOTION
MASSAGING ME WITH YOUR SMOOTH LOVE LOTION

EVERYTIME U ENTER
U MAKE ME FEEL TENDER
AND I SURRENDER
TO YOUR SOFT TOUCH
BABY U ARE TOO MUCH
GIVE IT TO ME WITH A SOUL TOUCH

U Getting Your Groove On

I SEE U ARE GETTING YOUR GROOVE ON
MR. WONDERMAN

RESTLESS NITE
NO SLEEP
SNEAKING OUT AT TWILIGHT
JUST TO PEEK FOR THE WEAK

SEARCHING FOR A HEART WITH NO FIGHT
WALKING AND PRETENDING
LIKE U GOT NO SIGHT
U HOOKED ON THE INTERNET CHAT
FISHING FOR LADIES THAT ARE PHAT
WHO IS DA BRAT?

U SO BUSY LOOKING FOR YOUR NEW CENTERFOLD
U PUT ME ON THE BACK BURNER
AND U SAY I AM TOO BOLD
NOW LET ME PUT YA ON HOLD!!!!!

I AM MUCH MORE THAN A PICTURE FRAME
I CAN NEVER BRING YA SHAME
I WILL NEVER LET MY PEN DOWN
AND TAKE UP YOUR GAME
ALL THE SAME
U ARE A PLAYA ON THE MOVE
MIND TEASER WITH A SLOW GROOVE
HOLDING BACK THE REAL U
WEARING A MASK TO TEASE A FEW

TURNING THEIR MIDNIGHTS INTO BLUE
WHEW WHEW
NOT I, NOT I BOO
I REFUSE TO STOOP LOW
AND TAKE A HARD BLOW

WONDERMAN YOUR INTEREST IS BELOW THE WAIST
AND EVEN IF U CUT AND PASTE
U CAN NEVER CONNECT
CAUSE I GOT YA IN CHECK
U CAN ONLY REFLECT
ON WHAT COULD HAVE BEEN

I CONTROL THIS SCENE
I WILL NEVER WASTE ANOTHER WORD ON U
REASON BEING U SUBTRACT FROM SOULS
AND ONLY DONATE TO A FEW
I AM OFF THIS FAKE INTERNET TRIP
DROP MY CHIP

Black Leather Couch Ouch

HEY BIG PAPA
LITTLE MAMMA IS ALL UP IN YA CRIB
LAYING UP ON YA BLACK COUCH OUCH

THE DOOR BELL RINGS
I ANSWER
A TALL SLIM BROTHER ENTERS
SPORTING NO TOP
CAUSE IT'S 90 DEGREES HOT

TRACK PANTS DRAPED NICELY
A LITTLE BAGGY
YOU TURNING ME ON BIG DADDY

I LOVE YOUR CRUNK IMAGE
MUSCLES WRIPPLING
PECKS SHINING
I MUST SAY YOU ARE TERRIBLY
INVITING

I AM INTO YOUR DARK CHOCOLATE FRAME
I AM FALLING FOR YOUR MASCULINE EDGE
AS YOU GREET ME WITH A PLEDGE

YOUR WORDS ROLL LIKE THIS
"BABY CAN YOU COMMIT TO THE CIRCUMSTANCE AT HAND"
I RESPOND " CAN YOU GET DOWN LIKE A REAL MAN"
MY REPLY "SSSSSSHHHHHH
NO NEED FOR WORDS
LETS GET IT ON
COME ON COME ON COME ON............

5th Avenue Penthouse

THIS ONE ON ONE
WILL MAKE ME COME
TO YOUR 5TH AVENUE PENTHOUSE
BOTTLE OF WINE IN HAND
AIMING TO FULLY ENTERTAIN MY MAN

GIVE ME THE ORDERS BABY
I WILL DROP MY TRENCH COAT ON COMMAND
MY BODY MASS IS YOUR TERRITORY
AND YOU ARE ABOUT TO CLAIM VICTORY

THIS ONE ON ONE
WILL HAVE NO INTERMISSION
THE EPISODES WILL BE LONG

RELAX HONEY
PREPARE YOURSELF FOR A MOUNTAIN
OF SUSPENSE
NO NEED TO FEEL TENSE

ARE U READY FOR A HOT BUBBLE BATH
ACCOMPANIED WITH A SCENTED OIL MASSAGE
STAY TUNED FOR THE BEGINNING AND THE AFTERMATH

MASQUERADE ALL OVER MY SATIN SKIN
I AM EQUIPPED FOR SOME DANGEROUS ENTERTAINING

TOGETHER WITH SOME SEXY DIALOGUE
I KNOW MY BABY
WILL KEEP MY BLOOD PUMPING

U Set the Pace

U SET THE PACE FOR THE MOOD I AM IN
U WAKE UP THE SOUL
DORMANT WITHIN MY MELANIN
U SET THE PACE FOR THE MOOD I AM IN
U STIR UP MY HOT CHOCOLATE
AND WHIP MY CREAM TO THE RIM
LET US SEE HOW DEEP WE CAN BOTH DIVE
OR CAN WE REALLY SWIM
JUMP IN
JUMP IN TO MY REALITY
GLIDE THROUGH MY CREATIVITY
LET THE GAMES BEGIN
AT THE END OF THIS MARATHON
WE BOTH WILL WIN
I WILL CROWN U KING
IF U CROWN ME QUEEN
ARE U GETTING THE PICTURE
I AM PAINTING THIS STEAMY SCENE
AFTER U DROP THAT ACE
I MIGHT JUST CHANGE POSITIONS
AND MAYBE I WILL SET THE PACE
SHUFFLE THAT DECK
ONE MORE TIME
LET ME SHOW U WHY I AM FINE
NOW REFLECT
ON WHY I AM YOUR COVER GIRL
AND WHY U WILL ALWAYS BE MY LOVER BOY
NOW THAT U HAVE BEEN SERVED
SHOW ME THE HAND I DESERVE

Who Am I

I AM MORE THAN WHAT MEETS THE EYE

I INVITE U BENEATH MY SKIN
TO GO BEYOND MY MELANIN
TO LOOK DEEP WITHIN

SCAN MY SOUL WITH YOUR RADAR LENSE
BRING ME TO A HALT AND TICKET ME

AFTER YOU'RE DONE
I WILL TELL U
ONE CITATION IS NOT ENOUGH
COME AT ME AGAIN
IF YOU FEEL U ARE TOUGH

IF U DARE TO WRITE ME UP
FOR INDECENT EXPOSURE OF MY SOUL
I WILL UNFOLD
LETTING U STRIP MY SOUL TO THE CORE

Sauvy, Sexy, Sultry, Klassy
& Incredibly Sassy

MS. KLASSY KAT
U PRETTY PHAT
& DEFINATELY HOT

Darling I like it when you talk to me like that

YOUR AIR IS SO DEBONAIR
& A LITTLE RARE

I WILL ONLY WAIT TO EXHALE
AS U BREATHE ME
AND I BREATHE U
AS WE CONNECT AS
2 BOO

TODAY I RECEIVE YOUR KOSMIC RAYS
AS I LAY ON TOP OF U HORIZONTALLY
AND U RESPONDTO ME VERTICALLY
I AM A DIVA
SO LET ME TASTE THAT FINE CHOCOLATE FLAVA
& LET ME FEEL YA FEVA

I WILL RECIPROCATE AND SHOW YA
WHY I AM THE SAUVY
SEXY
SULTRY
KLASSY AND
TRAIL BLAZING SASSY KINDA DIVA

Blaq Diamond

CAN A GURL GET A HUG
LONG DISTANCE WILL DO
CAN A GURL GIVE A HUG
IT IS ONLY FOR YOU
CAN A GURL ROLL UP ON YOU
WITH HER TOYS BIG BOY
CAN A GURL TANGLE
WITH A MAN THAT HAS GOT ANGLE
IF YOU ARE THE PERPENDICULAR
CAN THIS GURL BE YOUR HORIZONTAL
I AM READY FOR YOU BLAQ DIAMOND
IF IT IS A SHINE YOU ARE LOOKING FOR
YOU JUST FOUND SOME

Can You Handle This Situation At Large

THE SCENE IS SET
AND YOU ARE THE STAR BABY
YOU ARE HEATING UP MY SHEETS
AS YOU SCROLL BACK AND FORTH
AND UP AND DOWN
MAKING ME MOAN WITH A PURRING SOUND
AGAIN AND AGAIN YOU PARADE MY SOFT SKIN
MELTING MY BRONZE MELANIN

MY ROYAL BLOOD IS CHARGED
AND YOU ARE ABOUT TO HANDLE THIS SITUATION AT LARGE
KEEP IN MIND I AM TOP OF THE LINE
I AM MORE THAN A ONE NIGHT FLING
THIS QUEEN HAS THE HONEY
AND I GOT A MEAN STING
I WILL SEDUCE YOU WITH MY HONEY COMB
AND SEDUCE YOU TO COME ON HOME
I AM THE MOST DEBONAIR KITTY
YOU SURE YOU CAN HANDLE THIS SITUATION BABY
PLAY WITH ME
BUT CAN YOU SATISFY ME??????

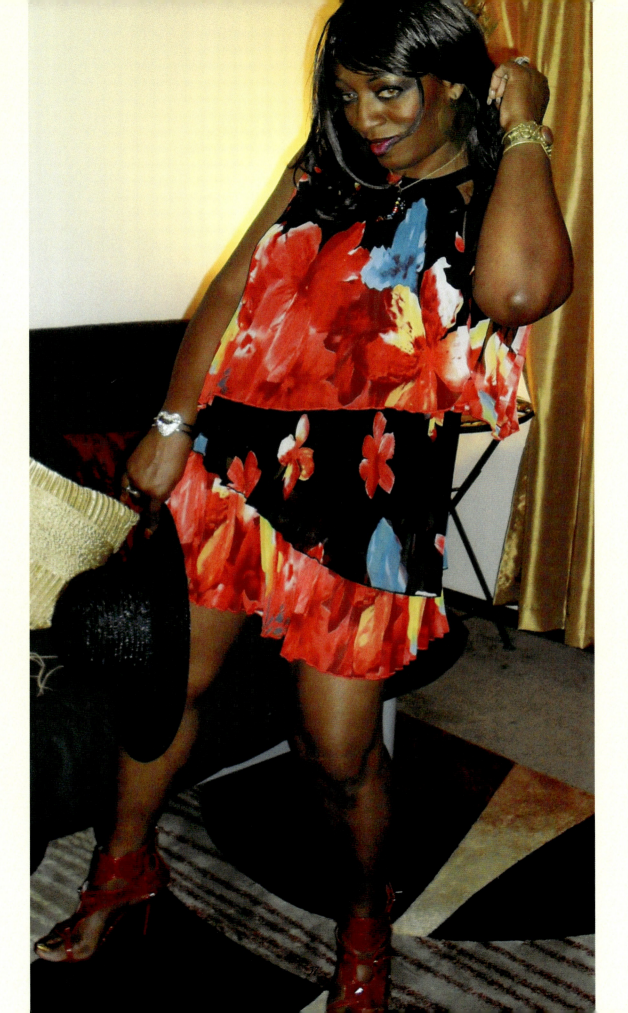

Sexy Strawberry Smoothie

DEEP RED SMOOTH ICY AND FIREY
I RESEMBLE A DELICIOUS STRAWBERRY SMOOTHIE
SEXY SEXY SEXY
HOMEMADE WITH A SIGNATURE OF GUAVA
DEFINING THE FINE FLAVA
RUNNING RINGS AROUND YOUR TASTE BUDS
SLOWLY MELTING
SLIDING DOWN YOUR THROAT
PLANNING TO GIVE YOU AN EARLY MORNING HIGH
LIPS KISSING EVERY SPOON
FEELING THE COOLEST OF COOL
I WILL BE HITTING YOU AGAIN AND AGAIN
WITH MY TANTALIZING CUP OF
DELICIOUS STRAWBERRY SMOOTHIE
RICH TANGY AND ALLURING

Wake Up
The Waters Of My Wetness

I AM LOOKING AT YOU AND YOU ARE LOOKING AT ME
I FEEL YOUR CURRENT
AS YOU STIR ME UP WITH AN OCEAN OF KISSES
YOU DIP INTO MY INWARD AND OUTWARD BEAUTIES
INTENDING TO WAKE UP THE WATERS OF MY WETNESS

WITH AN INVITATION TO SOME HOT LOVE
YOU PART MY LIPS WITH A KISS
IGNITING EMOTIONAL STATIC
WE ARE FLOWING REAL DEEP BABY
YOU ARE WAKING UP THE WATERS OF MY WETNESS

PLUGGING AND PLAYING
DIPPLING AND GLIDING
I AM LOVING YOUR MOVEMENTS
YOU ARE SO INFATUATING

YOU ARRANGE ME IN ASCENDING ORDER
1ST A GIGANTIC KISS ON MY LIPS
THEN A LITTLE TEASING BELOW MY HIPS
WAKING UP THE WATERS OF MY WETNESS

Red Hot Freestyle

COME CLOSER BABY
LET ME WHISPER THIS
POETIC JUSTICE IN YOUR EAR

BEEN CALLED SEXY LADY
DAILY
FROM THE TIME I HIT THE WORK PLACE DOOR
AND ON THE WEEKENDS
UP UNTIL I LEAVE THE DANCE FLOOR
I KNOW I CAN HANDLE MORE
BUT IT WOULD BE BETTER IF IT WAS COMING
FROM SOMEONE I ADORE

THAT IS YOU HONEY
MY LONG DISTANT CHERRY
RED AND DELICIOUS
AND AT TIMES DOUBLE BUBBLICIOUS

I FEEL YOU MOVING ALL UP IN MY POETIC IMAGINATION
A BIT FLIRTATIOUS
AND DEFINITELY NOT FICTITIOUS
CAN'T DENY I ENJOY YOU SO MUCH
AND AT THIS MOMENT I AM MISSING YOUR TOUCH

I INTEND TO TAKE AWAY THIS GAP
SO YOU CAN TAP DIRECTLY INTO ME
WANTING YOU BADLY
AND CRAVING YOU MADLY
I WANT US TO BE CLOSER AND CLOSER
AND EVENTUALLY FULL FLEDGE LOVERS

YOUR UNDERCOVER TROPICAL FLOWER

The planet is heating up and soul is at the core.

If you want more of her seductive heat, brace yourself for the next foot age.

Thanks once again for indulging in her captivating allure.

The chronicles continues..........

To correspond with Vivette Toni Davson A K A Deepblaqsoul you may write to her:

P. O. Box 3288

Decatur, GA. 30031

Email her at: perfumedwhispers@yahoo.com

indigopassions@yahoo.com

deepblaqsilohette@yahoo.com

or log on to her websites:

blackplanet.com

member name: deepblaqsoul

blackpeoplemeet.com

member name: soulfulessencefu

To purchase future books log on to Xlibris.com and type in name of book

Books are also on sale at: amazon.com and Barnes & Noble.com

Printed in the United States
By Bookmasters